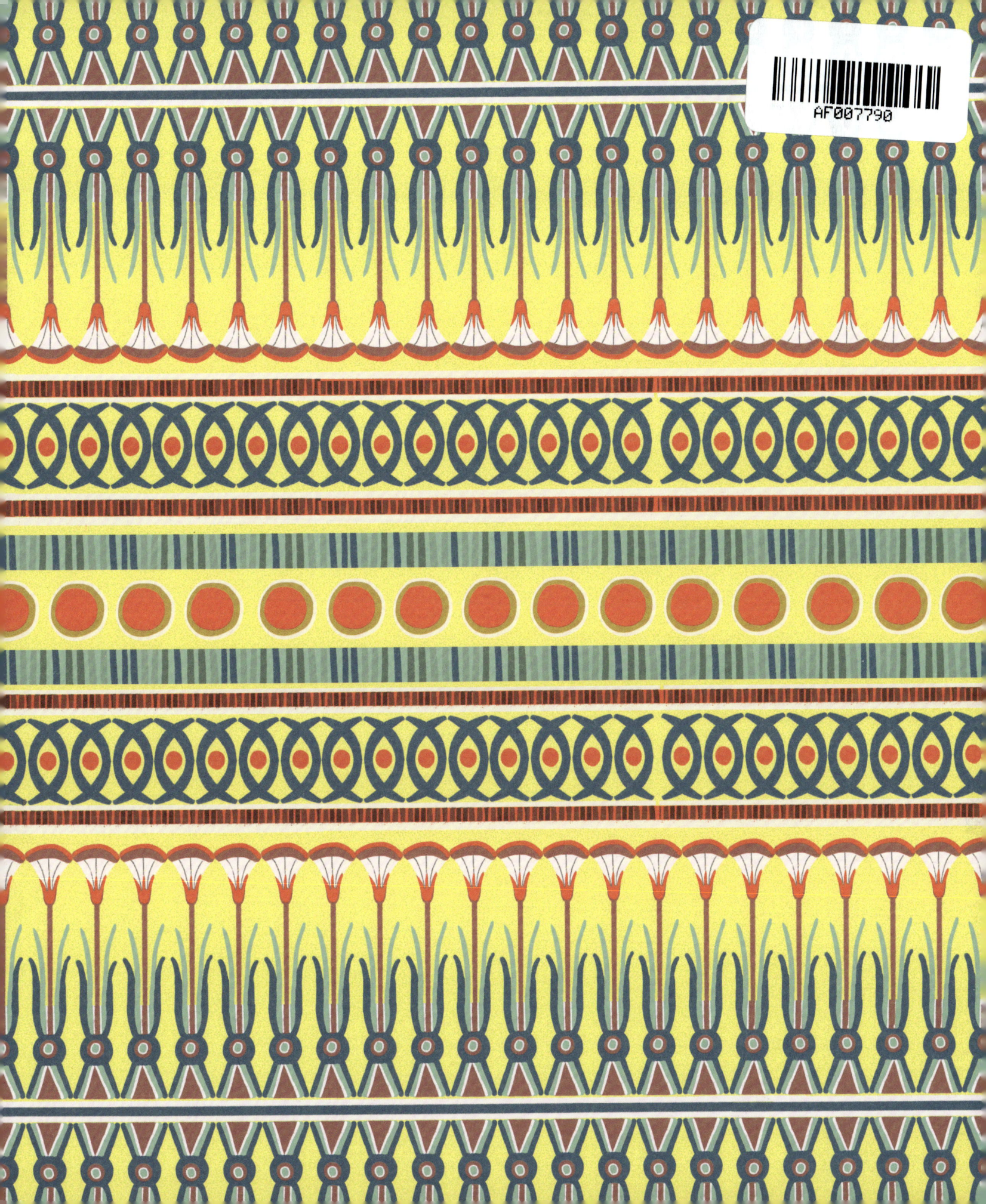

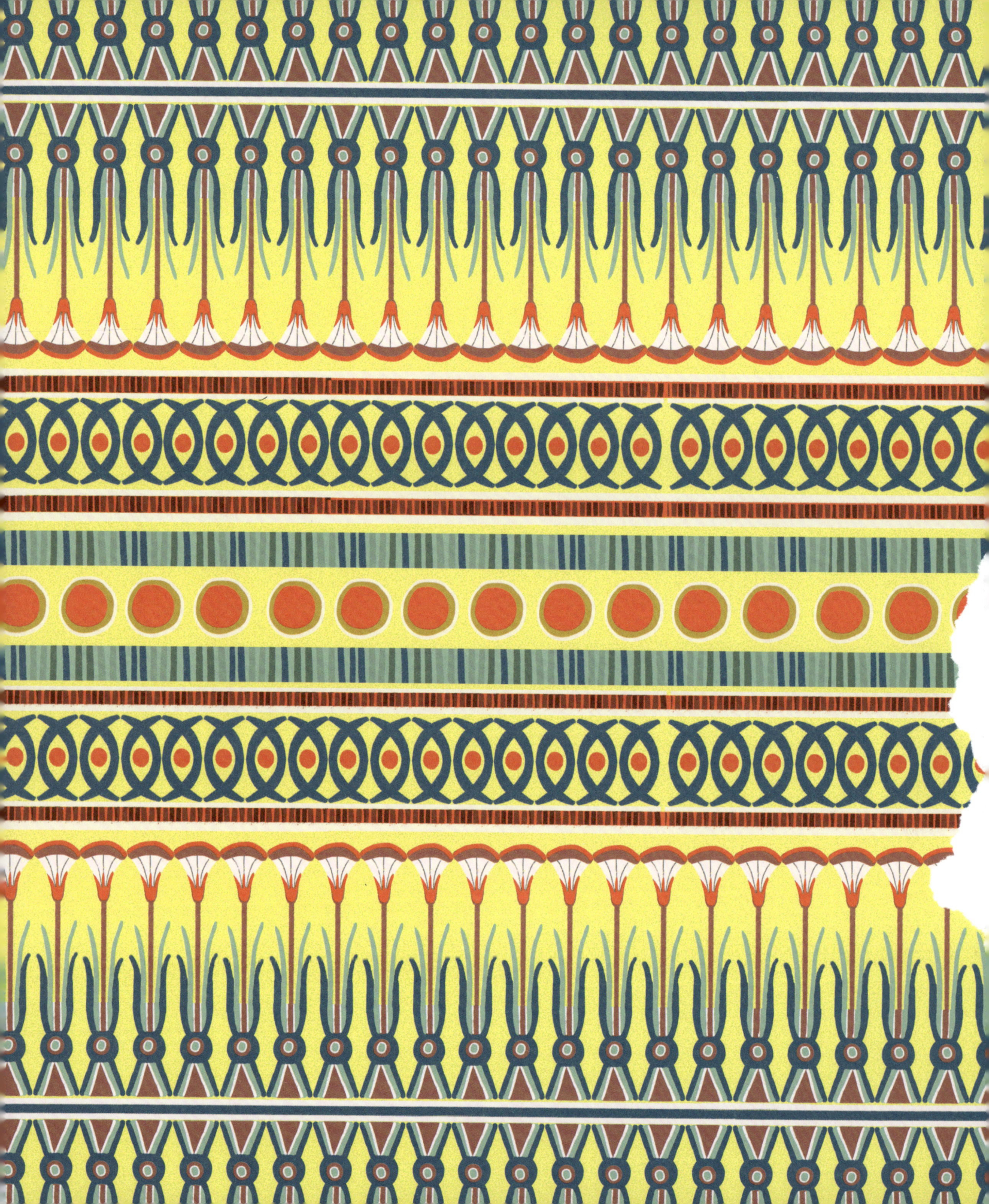

ANCIENT EGYPT
for children

illustrations by Javier Joaquín
texts by Paolo Marini

nuinui kids

Table of contents

Along the Nile: among the Hippos and Crocodiles *pages 4-5*
The Pyramids *pages 6-7*
The Great Sphinx *pages 8-9*
The Religion 1, 100, 1000 gods! *pages 10-11 and 12-13*
The Temple *pages 14-15*
The Pharaohs' Jewels *pages 16-17*
Make-up and Wigs *pages 18-19*
The Menu of Ancient Egyptians *pages 20-21*
Imhotep, the Little Scribe *pages 22-23*
The Worship of Animals *pages 24-25*
The Tomb of Pharaoh Seti I *pages 26-27*
Mummification *pages 28-29*

Secrets of the Mummies *pages 30-31*
The Mask of Tutankhamun *pages 32-33*
Senet, Fancy a Game? *pages 34-35*
The Book of the Dead and the Journey to the Afterlife *pages 36-37*
The Solar Barques *pages 38-39*
Rameses II, the King of Kings *pages 40-41*
Cleopatra, the Last Queen of Egypt *pages 42-43*
Tomb Raiders *pages 44-45*
Johnny the Archaeologist *pages 46-47*

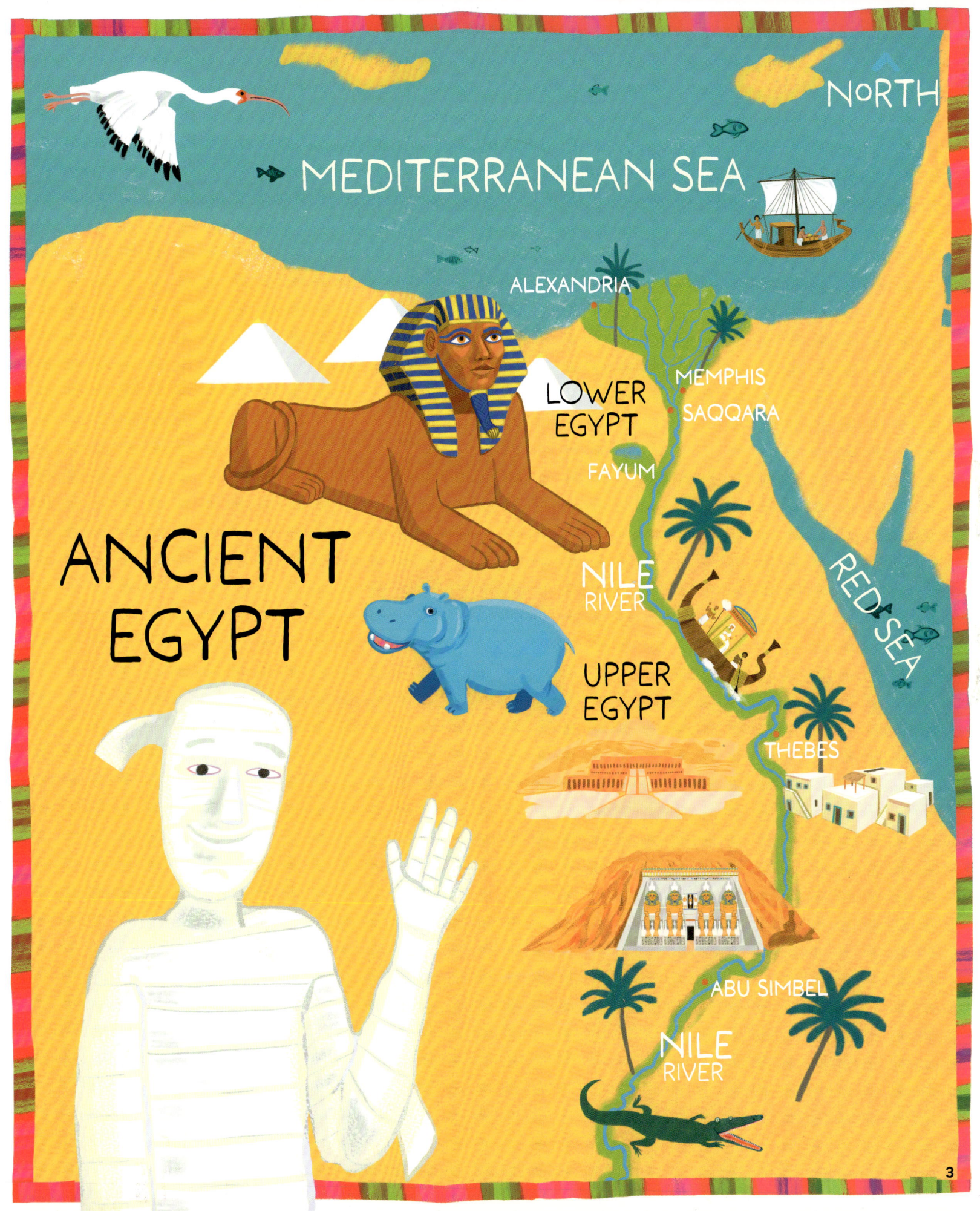

Along the Nile:

THE NILE RIVER IS ONE OF THE LONGEST IN THE WORLD: 6853 KILOMETRES!

The Nile flows across Egypt from south to north.

The ancient Egyptians owed their lives to the Nile. The river was essential for getting around, communicating and trading. Boats laden with people and goods travelled it daily.

among the Hippos and Crocodiles

Every year, the Nile overflows and the muddy waters cover the fields and make them fertile.

Hippos are aggressive animals; they can attack boats and people, so the Egyptians feared and respected them.

The Nile was home to many animals, such as crocodiles, hippos, and fish.

Among the Egyptian gods, there was a hippopotamus - the Goddess Taweret!

INSIDE THE GREAT PYRAMID WAS THE MUMMY OF PHARAOH KHUFU.

The pyramid was not built by slaves but by workers in the service of the Pharaoh.

It took over 2,000,000 huge stone blocks to build the Great Pyramid.

The Great Sphinx

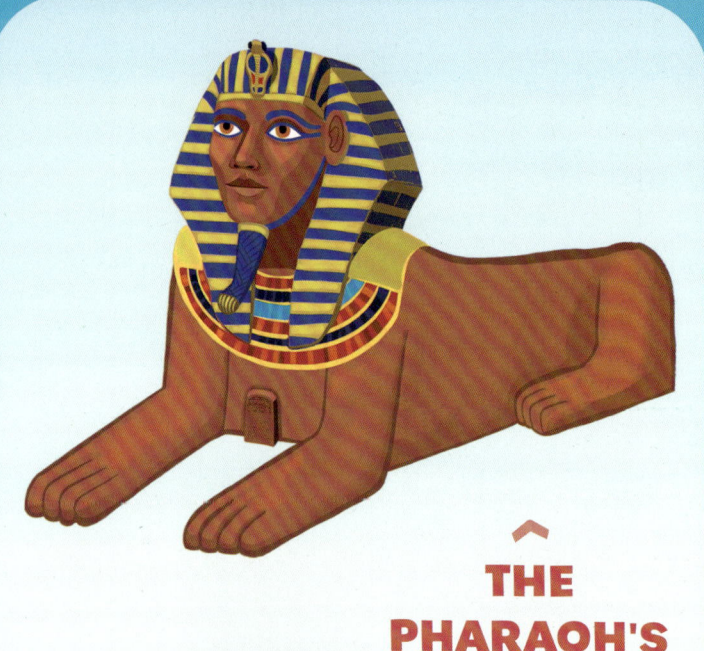

^ THE PHARAOH'S HEAD.

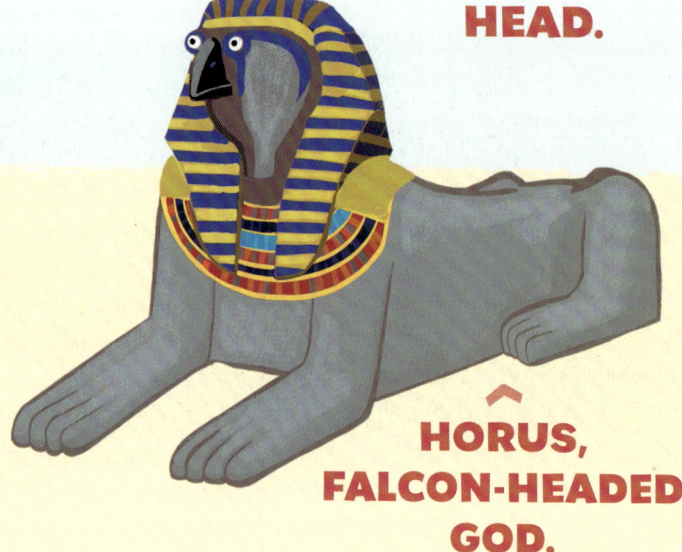

^ HORUS, FALCON-HEADED GOD.

AMUN, RAM-HEADED GOD.

The Sphinx is a fantastic creature with the body of a lion and the head of a person.

One story has it that **Pharaoh Thutmose** one day fell asleep between the legs of the Sphinx, which appeared to him in a dream and asked him to free it from the desert sands that covered it.

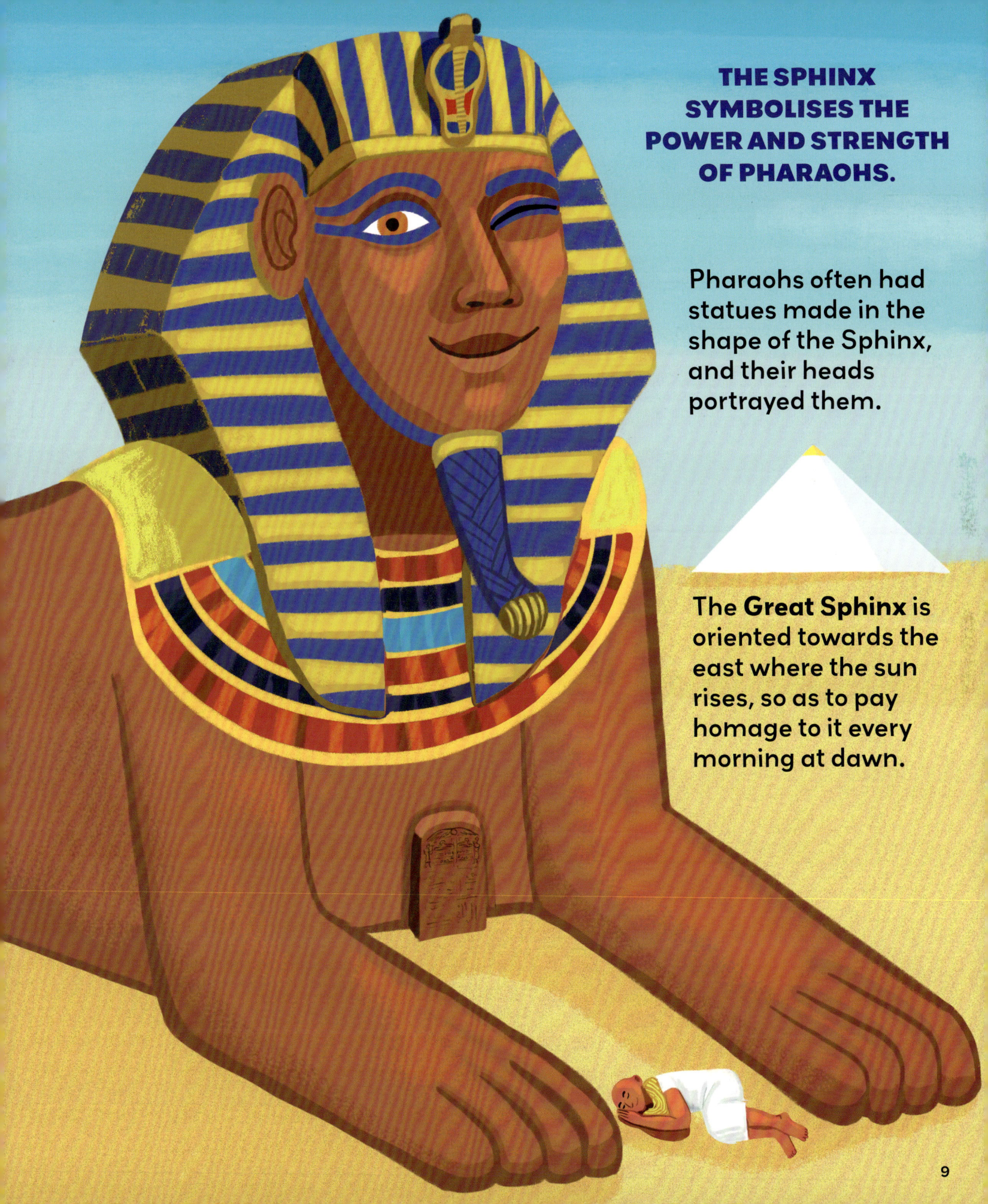

THE SPHINX SYMBOLISES THE POWER AND STRENGTH OF PHARAOHS.

Pharaohs often had statues made in the shape of the Sphinx, and their heads portrayed them.

The **Great Sphinx** is oriented towards the east where the sun rises, so as to pay homage to it every morning at dawn.

Egyptian Gods were many, at least 1500! They were human-like, animal-like or had human bodies and animal heads.

OSIRIS, LORD OF THE AFTERLIFE HAD GREEN SKIN. HE WAS DEAD AND THEN REBORN.

ISIS, the Goddess of magic and love, was mother of **HORUS**, the Falcon God, and wife of Osiris.

The Temple

Egyptian temples were made like telescopes; larger rooms on the outside getting smaller and smaller on the inside.

Only Pharaohs and priests could enter the temple; ordinary people could not.

Pharaoh ›

In temples, the columns represented plants, the floor was the earth, and the ceiling was the sky.

Inside the temples, a great many priests worked, each with a very specific task.

STATUES OF THE DEITY WERE CARED FOR LIKE LIVING PEOPLE.

THE MOST SACRED PLACE IN THE TEMPLE WAS WHERE THE STATUE OF THE DEITY STOOD.

Priests

The Pharaohs' Jewels

NOBLE EGYPTIANS WORE GOLD, SILVER, AND GEMSTONE JEWELLERY AND AMULETS, to adorn their bodies and, more importantly, to protect themselves from the demons of sickness.

Noblewomen wore long pleated robes, bracelets and anklets.

Queens could wear wreaths in the shape of vultures, the animal of the **GODDESS MUT.**

Their wigs were adorned with jewellery, tiaras and coloured beads.

The Pharaoh honoured worthy subjects with the '**gold of honour**' - a necklace made of golden discs.

The Pharaoh also gifted a gold pendant in the shape of a fly to the most valiant of men.

Egyptians believed that the skin of the Gods was made of gold, the bones of silver and the hair of lapis, all very precious elements.

Make-up

The nobility contoured their eyes with **kohl** to protect them from the desert sand and the sun's dazzling light.

Kohl was a black substance made of minerals, ash and animal fat.

NOBLES FOLLOWED FASHION AND ADORNED THEIR CLOTHES WITH LUXURIOUS FINERY.

Imhotep the Little Scribe

the one who can write

Egyptians made writing paper from papyrus plants, which grew in abundance along the Nile.

Little Imhotep learned the difficult art of Egyptian writing. He knew he would need many years of schooling to become a scribe.

Scribes used a tablet to mix the inks, a jar with ink and a nib.

Egyptians usually wrote from right to left, but you could also write from left to right and from top to bottom. **Never from bottom to top!**

Hieroglyphics are signs of Egyptian script considered divine.

The Worship of Animals

Ancient Egyptians believed certain animals to be Gods; they worshipped them and offered prayers to them.

Among the most mummified divine animals were: the **ibis** (a bird) **Thoth**, God of writing; the **crocodile Sobek**, God of the Nile; the **bull Apis**, sacred to the city of Memphis.

Among the most worshipped deities was Bastet, the Cat Goddess who protected the home, women and newborn children.

Many statues depict Bastet sitting like a cat on her hind legs, her tail rolled up and looking proud.

Many necropolises (**cemeteries**) for mummified divine animals have been found in Egypt.

At Abydos, for example, thousands of mummies of dogs have been discovered.

In addition to divine animals, the Egyptians sometimes had their own domestic animals mummified and placed in tombs.

Crocodiles, scorpions and beetles were worshipped and feared!

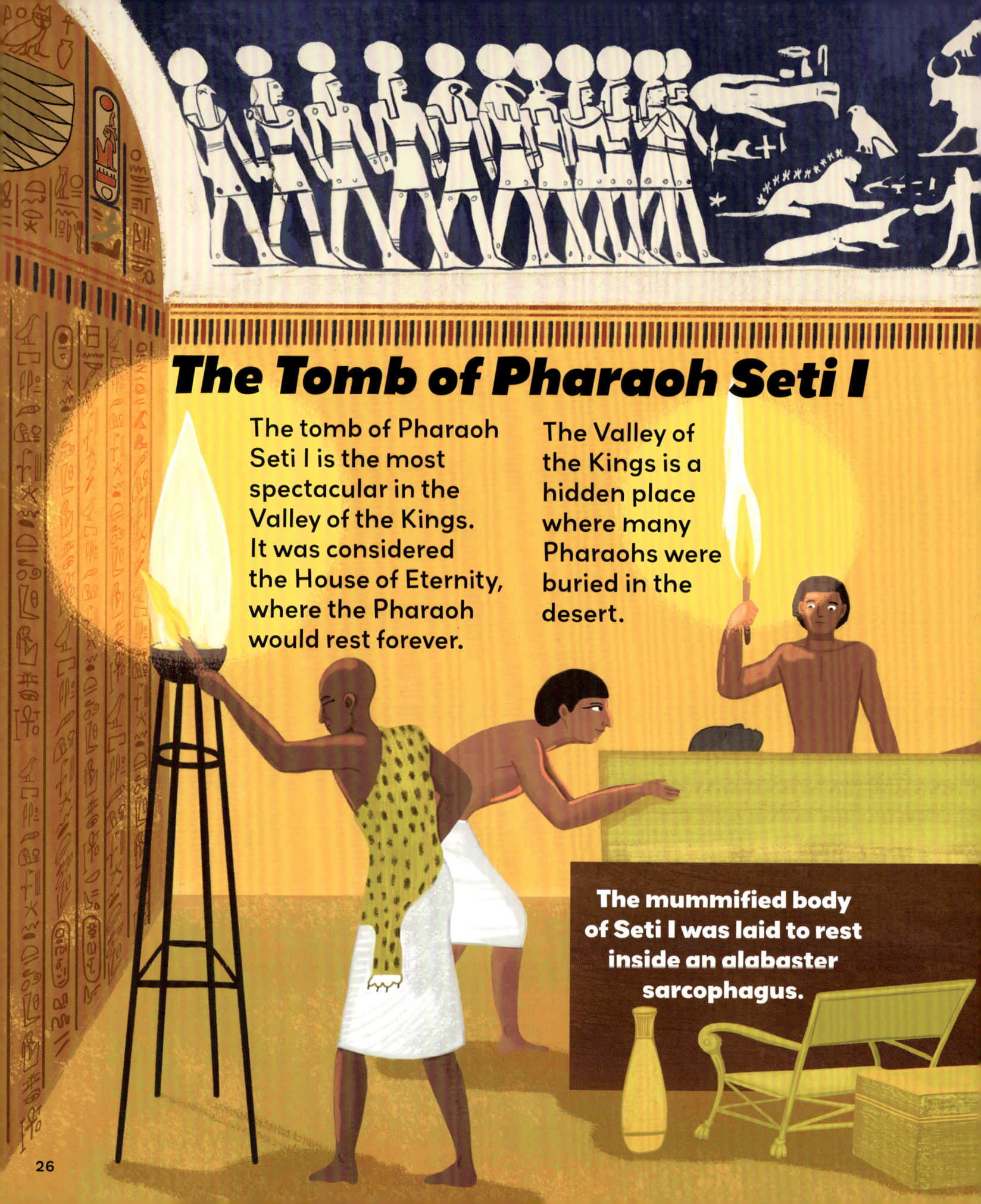

The Tomb of Pharaoh Seti I

The tomb of Pharaoh Seti I is the most spectacular in the Valley of the Kings. It was considered the House of Eternity, where the Pharaoh would rest forever.

The Valley of the Kings is a hidden place where many Pharaohs were buried in the desert.

The mummified body of Seti I was laid to rest inside an alabaster sarcophagus.

Seti I reigned for about 15 years. With a large army, he reorganised and conquered many territories.

After death, all the exquisite objects in the Pharaoh's tombs were used in the afterlife.

The heavens are on the ceiling of Seti I's tomb, with the stars forming the Egyptian constellations.

THE TOMB OF SETI I WAS FIRST DISCOVERED IN 1817 BY GIOVANNI BATTISTA BELZONI FROM PADUA, AN ADVENTURER CALLED 'THE GIANT OF THE NILE'.

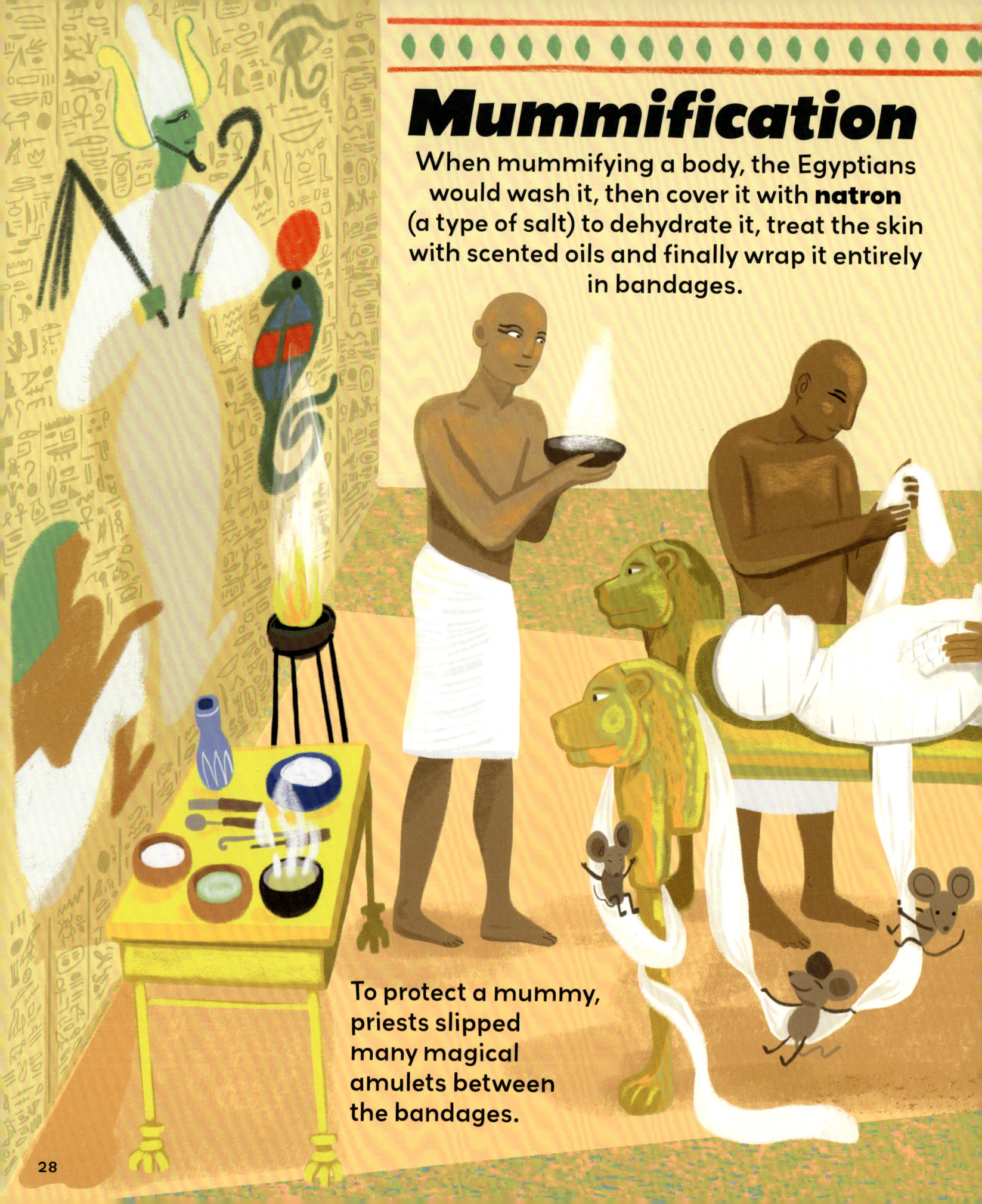

Mummification

When mummifying a body, the Egyptians would wash it, then cover it with **natron** (a type of salt) to dehydrate it, treat the skin with scented oils and finally wrap it entirely in bandages.

To protect a mummy, priests slipped many magical amulets between the bandages.

Their liver, lungs, stomach and intestines were mummified separately and placed inside containers called '**canopic jars**'.

Hearts, believed to be the most significant organ, were mummified and then replaced in the body. On the other hand, brains were taken out and thrown away.

CANOPIC JARS were shaped like the four sons of Horus: Imsety, Hapy, Duamutef and Qebehsenuef. They were funerary deities who protected the organs of the deceased.

IMSETY: HUMAN HEAD

HAPY: BABOON HEAD

QEBEHSENUEF: FALCON HEAD

DUAMUTEF: JACKAL HEAD

The God of mummification was Anubis, a man with a canine head. He was often seen wandering around Egyptian tombs in the desert.

Secrets of the Mummies

COVERED WITH MAGIC FORMULAS, SARCOPHAGI PROTECTED MUMMIES FROM THE DEMONS OF ROT.

Egyptians believed that when a person died, their soul would fly out of their body in the form of a bird bearing a human head.

Sarcophagi may have looked like the deceased. If a mummy got damaged, a sarcophagus would take its place.

Egyptians believed that for the deceased to live on in the afterlife, their bodies had to remain intact, which is why they were mummified.

Ancient Egyptians also believed that people lived on after death in a world parallel to their earthly one.

Mummies were regarded as deities. For the Egyptians, they were sacred and immortal.

Did you know that Pharaoh Ramesses II's mummy has a passport? It's true!

He used it to go to France, where he could recover from an illness affecting him!

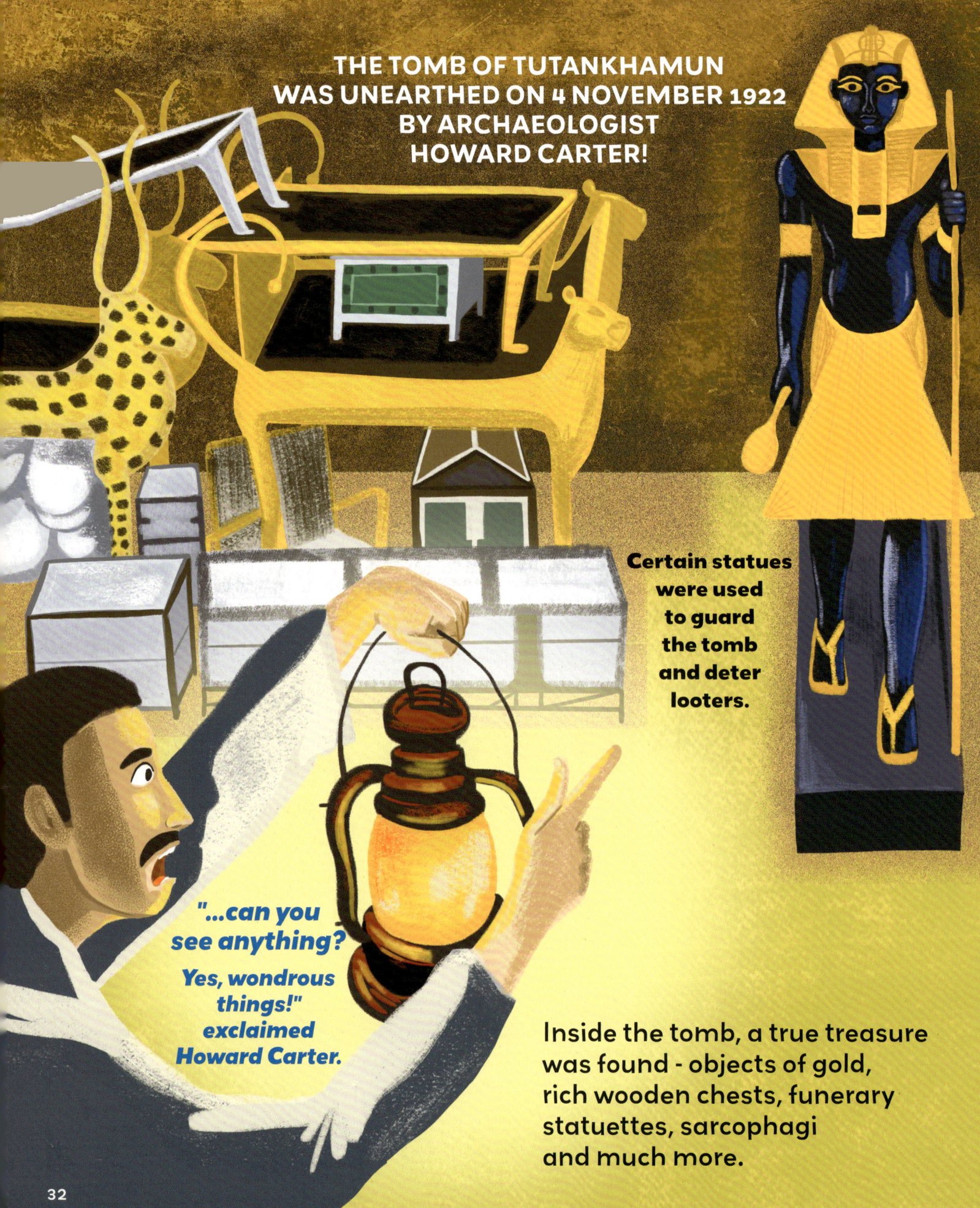

The Mask of Tutankhamun

Tutankhamun became Pharaoh when he was only 11 years old. That is why he is called the Child Pharaoh.

What a bizarre headdress! In fact, this is a Nemes headdress that only Pharaohs could wear!

A funerary mask weighing 18 kg of gold and precious stones was placed on the Pharaoh's face.

Tutankhamun's mummy was protected by eight large sarcophagi, all magnificently decorated.

Sadly, Tutankhamun died very young, and his tomb was finished quickly.

Senet,
Fancy a game?

Senet means **'to pass'**. It's a bit of a mysterious game. All we know is that it's similar to "Snakes and Ladders" and Backgammon.

The pawns in senet are called 'dancers' and the squares 'houses'.

Senet was not only played in Egypt but throughout the Mediterranean. It is among the earliest known games.

NEFERTARI

Even in the afterlife, they played Senet. If a deceased person won, they could meet God Ra and be born to a new life.

In many tombs, the Egyptians were depicted playing Senet with the Deities. Thoth, the wisest of the Gods, was the hardest to beat.

GOD THOTH

If Queen Nefertari succeeded in beating Thoth, her spirit, the Bird-ba, would survive and soar into the afterlife.

The Book of the Dead
and the Journey to the Afterlife

The Egyptian afterlife was envisioned as a place full of dangers. This is why the deceased carried a 'Book of the Dead', a papyrus scroll with magic formulas for overcoming adversities.

Reaching the afterlife, the deceased faced the judgement of God Osiris. Their heart was weighed on a scale. It had to be lighter than a feather to pass the test.

OSIRIS

HORUS

weighing of the heart

The Solar Barques

According to legend, when the God Ra became too old to reign over the Earth, the Goddess Nut turned into a celestial cow to lift him onto her back. When Nut raised Ra above the Earth, she became the sky and Ra the King of the Gods.

God Ra resembled a man with the head of a falcon and a sun disc on top.

RA

According to belief, Ra crossed the sky in his barque every day.

Nile River

Rameses II
the King of Kings

Rameses II is one of the best-known Pharaohs in history. He reigned for many years and built numerous monuments.

THE PHARAOH HAD MANY WIVES, BUT ONLY ONE WAS THE QUEEN. HER NAME WAS NEFERTARI. RAMESSES DEDICATED MANY TEMPLES AND THE MOST SPLENDID TOMB IN THE VALLEY OF THE QUEENS TO HER.

For the Egyptians, obelisks symbolised petrified rays of the sun. They were tipped with gold and inscribed with royal titles. Ramesses had many of them made.

Ramesses II is said to have had more than 100 sons, but he only had one successor named **Merneptah**!

One of Ramesses' best-known temples is the one he built at Abu Simbel, protected by four colossal statues of the Pharaoh.

Cleopatra the Last Queen of Egypt

Cleopatra VII was the last queen of Pharaonic Egypt. Upon her death, the Nile Valley became a province of the Roman Empire.

Cleopatra was very charming, spoke many languages and was very intelligent. First, Julius Caesar and then Mark Antony fell in love with her.

Mark Antony swore eternal love to Cleopatra.

The Romans were very jealous of Cleopatra, so they came up with many untrue stories.

They said she was evil, practised black magic and tortured slaves.

When Cleopatra was defeated by the Romans, to avoid suffering the humiliation of being taken to Rome in chains, she took her own life.

Cleopatra died when she was bitten by an asp, a very poisonous snake.

Tomb Raiders

To stop tomb raiding, the Pharaohs of the New Kingdom had their tombs hidden in the desert. Today, these places are called the Valley of the Kings and the Valley of the Queens.

The tombs of the Pharaohs were not full of traps and cursed.

They were tightly sealed and their location kept a secret to ward off thieves.

EVEN IN ANTIQUITY, TOMB RAIDERS CAUGHT BY THE GUARDS WERE SEVERELY PUNISHED.

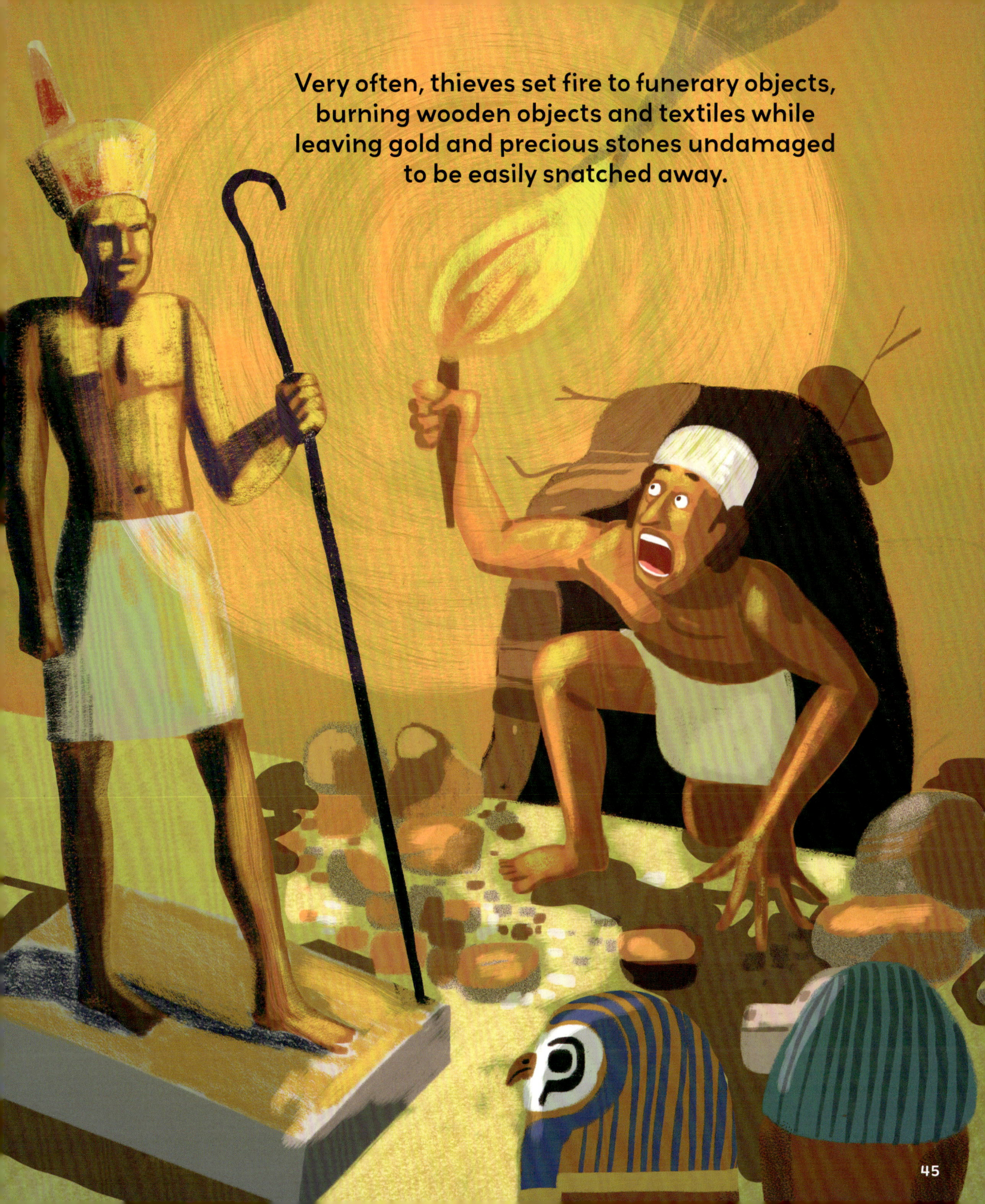
Very often, thieves set fire to funerary objects, burning wooden objects and textiles while leaving gold and precious stones undamaged to be easily snatched away.

Johnny the Archaeologist

These objects are very fragile, so you have to be very careful, take lots of photographs, and examine the surroundings.

To distinguish the layers, you have to look closely at the colour of the earth and its texture.

Any objects found in an excavation are immediately studied in a tent with all the necessary tools to analyse them.

To do a good job, an archaeologist has to study the layers of the ground one by one.

By doing this, he can date the artefacts he finds.

Paolo Marini

After graduating and getting a PhD in Egyptology, he has worked on many excavations in Egypt and the Near East. For years, he has worked with renowned museums and written scientific articles and books for adults and children.

Javier Joaquín

Born in Buenos Aires, Argentina, he discovered his vocation for drawing and painting early on. He always starts with a pencil sketch and then works with textures and colours both traditionally and digitally. His passion for fine arts, his curiosity for nature, and his degree in Psychology have provided him with a unique perspective that defines his creative work.

Ancient Egypt for children
© Nuinui SA 2024
nuinui kids® is a registered trademark belonging to Nuinui SA
Chemin du Tsan du Pèri, 10, 3971 Chermignon - Switzerland
Translation : Marissa Frost
All rights of translation, reproduction and full or partial adaptation and with any means are reserved for all countries.
ISBN 978-2-88975-453-3
Printed in China

www.nuinui.it

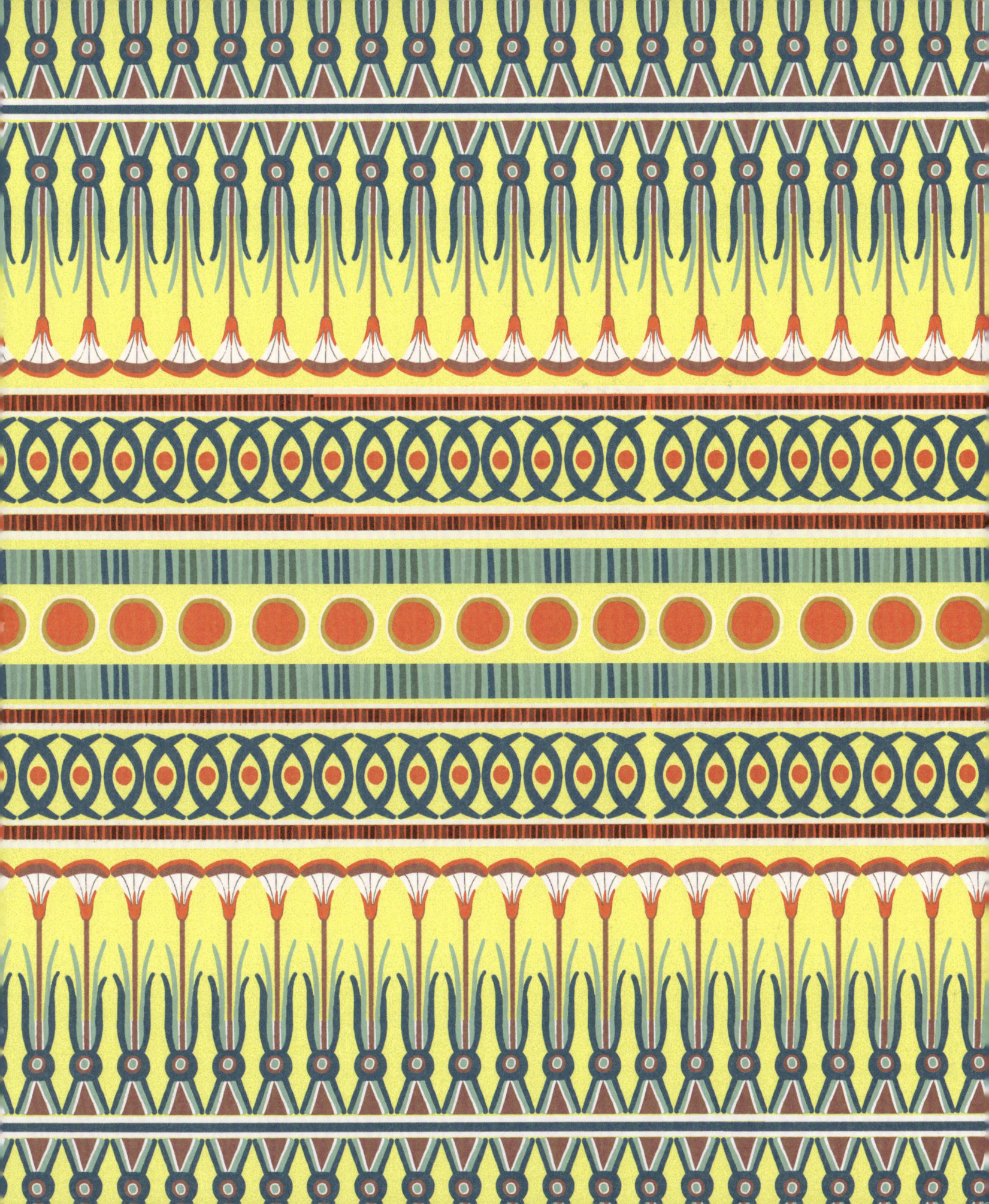